The P

by Karen Williamson
Illustrated by Sarah Conner

CANDLE
BOOKS

Jesus told lots of stories to show that God cares for us and loves us.

One story was about a farmer who had two sons.

"I want to leave home!" said the younger son one day. "Please give me all my money!"

The young man took a long journey
to a far country.

Soon the boy had packed his bag and set off. His father was very sad to see him go.

When he arrived, he spent his money
giving lots of parties.

But before long all the money had gone.

As soon as the money went, his friends disappeared too.

Now the younger son had no money and no food.

The only job he could find was feeding muddy, greedy pigs.

He was so hungry he even felt like eating the pigs' food!

Finally he came to his senses.
"Dad has servants who are much better off than me," he thought.

So he decided to go home.
It was a long, weary journey.

At last he saw his house.
His father was watching out for him.

While he was still a long way off,
his father saw him.

The old man was so happy!
He ran to meet his lost son.

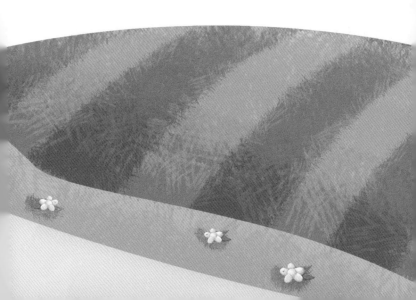

He hugged and kissed his lost son.
"Father, I have done wrong!" said the boy.

"I left my family and wasted your money.
I'm not good enough to be your son."

His father stopped him.
"Quick!" he shouted to his servants.
"Bring out the best clothes for my son!"

"Tell cook to roast the best calf!
We're having a great feast to celebrate."

"This son of mine was lost –
but now he's found!"

They had such a party!

"God is happy too," said Jesus, "when he welcomes home people who are lost."